REFLECTIONS
A DAILY DOSE OF INSPIRATION

MICHELLE LEACOCK

ASCEND
PUBLISHERS

Ascend Publishers
Metuchen, New Jersey 08840
www.ascendpublishers.com

Reflections
Copyright © 2009 by Michelle Leacock

ISBN: 13: 978-0-615-30327-7

All scripture quotations, unless otherwise indicated, are taken from the Holy Bible: Thinline Bible, New International Version® . Copyright © 1996 by International Bible Society.

Interior and cover design by 4EVERGRAFIX.

Printed in the United States of America

INTRODUCTION

I am truly delighted you are holding this book in your hands. It's been a long time coming. As simple as it looks, my journey here was a painful, yet delightful one—not because writing is difficult for me, but because discipline was. Every time I sat down to write, I became crippled with voluminous thoughts that kept me dreaming; dreaming of ways I can organize the content herein, what I should title each entry, whom I might offended or inspire. The list goes on. So, I would take a break—a few weeks here, a few there, until months and years went by. I'd frequent local bookstores in hopes of being inspired only to find new releases with the very thoughts and ideas that flooded my mind at some point or another. Then I'd convince myself that every idea I'd ever had about writing, had already been penned. So why bother?

Then, along came a friend, who would convince me that I do in fact have a voice worth hearing. He encouraged me to start a daily blog to develop discipline. Though it was not daily, it worked. I began writing on a more consistent basis and I realized that while I might have similar ideas to others, no one can tell my story or share my experiences quite like me. And so my journey as a writer now begins. I hope you are blessed by reading Reflections.

ACKNOWLEDGEMENTS

This book would not be possible without the most obvious of helpers, The Holy Spirit, and so I thank God. I'd also like to thank those individuals who have contributed in some way or another; my sister, Mary, for recognizing my writing before I did, Karl, the friend who told me I had a voice and encouraged me to begin blogging as a way to develop discipline, Ernst, my designer, for "putting up" with me, Linda and Ron, for your creative eyes and for providing your resources to me in a pinch, Kim, Elaine, Gwen, Debbie, my sister, Judy, for being early supporters, Jackie for your publishing expertise and advice, Angie, for all that you do, Kim, my editor, and last but not least, my fiancé, Anthony, for your patience, guidance, and input. I love you all. God bless you.

DAY 1

"A gift opens the way for the giver and ushers him into the presence of the great"
(Proverbs 18:16)

Many of us are part of a cultic following of the American Idol phenomenon. Each of us for different reasons plans his or her schedule around this broadcast, or rather, this EVENT.

The contestants make us laugh, cry, cheer, sing and sometimes gnash our teeth in agony. Whatever the effect on us, we ultimately enjoy it. The infamous Simon gets a lot of flack for verbalizing everyone's mental commentary when the vocally challenged howls in the wind. The sad truth is that these hopefuls really think they have the gift of singing and were probably encouraged by someone who was either tone deaf or afraid of being as truthful as Simon. The reality is these individuals aren't completely mistaken because they are in fact very talented—just not in the area of singing. Somehow, somewhere, they missed it.

Each of us is born for greatness in very specific areas. Some of us are aware of our areas of greatness; some of us aren't; and some of us have lost it along the way, perhaps because we have allowed someone to talk us out of it. Then, there are those who have decided that they prefer another path than that which has been predestined for them. At some point or another I have operated in each of these categories, but destiny has its grip on me. You see, I was born to write, to inspire, to create. My journey, however, has taken me in various directions that have eventually led me back to destiny. And here I am.

I thought that I had to write only best-sellers to be successful as a writer. So I got stuck trying to come up with concepts that I thought would sell when I should have just put pen to paper and asked for divine guidance in purposeful writing—regardless of the outlet. This truth hit me one day during a visit with a friend. We listened to a speech about purpose by a former talk-show host, and the summation of it is this: Everything we need to walk out our purpose is already in us. Stop waiting for the "right time," and stop making a host of other excuses. The time is now. There are people that your particular gift, executed by your hands (by the grace of God), is supposed to impact.

Those people are waiting on you, and you will have to answer just like the man who hid his talent in *Matthew 25: 14-30*. I understand this parable better now because I started a blog to develop the discipline of writing every day and to inspire others. I once missed a post thinking that no one would notice. But soon after I received an e-mail from my sister stating that she had spread the word and folks were awaiting their daily inspirational reading. That was music to my ears. While I believe I will write best-sellers someday, I will enjoy the journey getting there. DON'T KEEP THEM WAITING!

Personal Reflection

Am I using my gifts?

_____

_____

_____

_____

_____

_____

_____

_____

_____

_____

_____

_____

_____

DAY 2

"What good is it for a man to gain the whole world, yet forfeit his soul"
(Mark 8:36)

There was a period in my life where I could not recall the last time I prayed—truly prayed. At best, I had mentally acknowledged God while running out the door. And church had become more of an activity than an anticipated time of worship and spiritual rejuvenation.

My focus had been on the pursuit of a new home and job. I figured that as soon as I found my new home and job I would get back to nurturing my relationship with God. I had to keep reminding myself that gratitude for whatever I have in any given moment is key to achieving what lies ahead. It's pointless for us to reach a goal without the perspective of how we got there. While focusing on where we want to be instead of where we are, the enemy of our soul uses every moment to further his plan to destroy us.

So be reminded of how important it is to get fully clothed in the full armor of God: the belt of truth, which holds a soldier's weapons; the breastplate of righteousness, which protects the soldier's heart; the footwear of readiness, which aids in a firm stance; the shield of faith, which repels opposing objects; the helmet of salvation, which protects from a higher angle of attack; and the sword of the Spirit, which penetrates and ultimately destroys the enemy.

Being fully clothed in the armor of God is not like our earthly activity of getting dressed once or twice a day. It takes discipline and commitment to studying, believing, and meditating on the Word. It is essentially, a lifestyle.

Personal Reflection

Is there a crack in my armor?

_____

_____

_____

_____

_____

_____

_____

_____

_____

_____

_____

_____

_____

DAY 3

"Mercy, peace and love be yours in abundance"
(Jude 1 :2)

So often we go about our day oblivious to our very breath, the pounding of our hearts, the blood that flows through our veins and our organs that operate in divine symphony. Then, something happens—either good or bad—to remind us of just how precious life is.

Some time ago while recovering from a dark moment, which kept me from feeling my own heartbeat, a good friend of mine called me to share that God had entrusted her to bring two lives into the world at the same time. How awesome that the human body is capable of such a thing! I was thrilled and honored to be among her supporters. I had to pause and meditate on how life continues whether or not we participate because while I was wallowing in my troubles and neglecting to enjoy life's journey—life continued.

That same evening I received the devastating news that my sixteen-year old niece was diagnosed with a rare form of cancer that had so far affected only one percent of our nation's population. This was a vicious reminder that life as we know it has an eventual end. However, as it would turn out, the end of my niece's life is not to be now. After being jolted out of my false reality that the enemy was winning, I, along with friends, family, and the backing of God's angels, banded together to lift up a standard against this cruel attack. We didn't know how or when God would deliver. We just knew He would. Four days later after a series of rigorous tests by specialists, we were told that the lump that had been removed from my niece just one week prior contained all the cancerous cells that were in her body. No chemo therapy or radiation was necessary. All she needed was a healing touch from Jesus.

No matter the length of life on this earth, it is to be lived in abundance. Each day should be lived to glorify our Creator. Only then can we truly experience what it means to live in abundance.

Personal Reflection

What's preventing me from living in abundance?

_____

_____

_____

_____

_____

_____

_____

_____

_____

_____

_____

_____

_____

_____

DAY 4

"For I know the plans I have for you, declares the Lord, plans to prosper you and not to harm you, plans to give you hope and a future"
(Jeremiah 29:11)

How often have we heard, "Those who fail to learn from their past are doomed to repeat it?" While there is great merit in this statement, overanalyzing it can be detrimental.

A few years ago I wrestled with a major decision. I looked at the pros and cons from every angle, logically and spiritually. I reached out to those I believe God has placed in my life to provide wisdom. My struggle at the time was figuring out whether I was hearing the voice of God or the voice of doubt speaking to me from past experiences. Within a twelve hour span I had changed my mind over ten times because I was afraid—afraid that what happened to me in the past might happen again. "Breathe," I told myself, "just breathe."

I called my brother and sister several times and must have annoyed them in my moments of fear and contemplation. Then, I read an article which sent me further into a tailspin. I soon asked myself the tough question: What are you afraid of? My initial answer was that I was afraid of missing God. While this was true, I knew it was just the surface. So, I dug deeper and found that not only was I afraid of missing God but was also afraid of not having enough, of not being good enough or wise enough to push beyond my past experiences.

I have been told many times that I'm blessed with a mind that is predisposed to genius. Yet, I tend to use this same mind to overanalyze a situation, thinking of the worse case scenario. I've learned that while misfortunes and detours in life can seem horrific, allowing them to cripple me and to make me afraid to move on is not an option. I know that I am well-equipped and favored for a great future because God said so.

We can choose to see God in nothing, in some things, or in everything, which allows us to actively rest in the assurance that He is faithful and that He wants the very best for His children. We can turn our fears over to Him or allow them to paralyze us. The choice is ours.

Personal Reflection

What fears am I allowing to paralyze me?

_____

_____

_____

_____

_____

_____

_____

_____

_____

_____

_____

_____

_____

DAY 5

"God opposes the proud but gives grace to the humble"
(James 4:6)

About four years ago I was away on an extended business trip. It was a particularly busy time for me because I was balancing business travel with my graduate studies. I had returned home after this trip to find a letter from my auto insurance company stating that my policy had lapsed. Since it was only ten days after the payment due date, and I had the policy for almost eight years, I confidently assumed that I could call my agent and straighten things out. I was told in order to reinstate my policy I would have to pay the new rate which was sixty percent higher than the rate I was paying at the time. Needless to say, after bellowing a few choice words to the agent, I did not renew my policy.

What happened to my grace period? This is the time given to rectify an error if by chance you failed to remember to do or pay something. According to dictionary.com, grace is an allowance of time after a debt or bill has become payable granted to the debtor before suit can be brought against him or her or a penalty applied. In other words, we pay for this kind of grace, which is not to be confused with the grace of God.

How many times have we found ourselves wondering why God has not brought judgment on our neighbor or co-worker for offending us or causing us distress or for what we perceive to be intentional harm? After all, as His children, isn't He supposed to come to our defense when we call? Never mind His delayed judgment on us for cutting someone off on the highway or for gossiping about the praise and worship team that did not do a good job ushering in the Holy Spirit on Sunday. And the list goes on.

God's grace is freely given and unmerited. We need not pay a premium or avoid accidents to receive His grace. And to top it off, His grace extends way beyond ten days. Don't believe me? Think about one thing or situation that you know God has been calling you out of and has been warning you time and time again to set aside and to follow Him. How long ago should He have brought judgment on you but has decided to extend His grace to you instead?

Though God is longsuffering with us and though His mercy and grace never run out, there comes a time when He must allow us to deal with the consequences of our ways so that we learn the lesson set before us and grow spiritually. He loves us just the way we are, yet He loves us too much to leave us in the same broken state. We are not to abuse His grace but rather to understand that "grace" is really the period of time between our awareness of our wrongdoing and repentance. Let us use God's grace period to do what we know is right.

Personal Reflection

Am I in God's grace period?

_____

_____

_____

_____

_____

_____

_____

_____

_____

_____

_____

_____

DAY 6

"If I go up to the heavens, you are there; if I make my bed in the depths, you are there"
(Psalm 139:8)

In 1998, a movie entitled *The Truman Show* hit the silver screen. Unbeknownst to the main character, every minute of his life was being recorded and displayed for the nation's entertainment.

What if unbeknownst to you, your life was being recorded for one month? What would the cameras see? Would there be a common theme? Would your audience be able to determine what you value most or gauge your moral barometer? Would your private life be consistent with what you publicly display?

Some of us live our lives in duality—saint-like in public yet uninhibited behind closed doors—and have quite possibly mastered this ability. However, the reality is that our lives are in fact being recorded and He who sees in the dark will certainly hold us accountable. Even if we are able to deceive the people in our lives, we cannot deceive God, the all-knowing one. There is no place we can go to escape His eyes. He's watching our every move.

Personal Reflection

Am I living a double life?

_____

_____

_____

_____

_____

_____

_____

_____

_____

_____

_____

_____

_____

DAY 7

"I am the vine; you are the branches. If a man remains in me and I in him, he will bear much fruit; apart from me you can do nothing"
(John 15:5)

Over the past decade there has been an increased interest in the consulting sector and personal wealth-creation. Recently, I've been in the company of several individuals who have become focused on either starting their own businesses or using various opportunities to create what's referred to as multiple streams of income. Individuals from CEOs to mailroom clerks are moonlighting as cosmetics and life insurance sales representatives, for example. I find this admirable, and I am in the process of assessing my own options. However, I am beginning to notice my own obsession of wanting to be in control of my life's direction.

While being ambitious and proactive about one's future is important and demonstrates the outer working of our God-given gifts and talents, it is equally important that the streams of income we create are connected to the main source—God.

The definition of stream is a body of water with a detectable current, confined within a bed and bank. If the streams of income we create are not connected to The Source, the profits are limited. The definition of a river is a natural waterway that flows from higher ground to lower ground. If we view God as our river, the Source to which the streams are connected, we can begin to understand that unless our "multiple streams of income" are connected to Him and His purpose, there can never be a steady flow.

As believers in Christ, we cannot selectively decide which parts of our lives to surrender to God. It's all or nothing. So as we pursue our dreams, we must be careful to assess them in light of scripture. Our streams must remain connected to the River that flows infinitely.

Personal Reflection

Am I attempting success without God?

DAY 8

"Therefore, there is now no condemnation for those who are in Christ Jesus"
(Romans 8:1)

A dear friend of mine once expressed to me his intent to right all the wrongs he had done in his past, particularly those that have impacted his children. While he claimed he had repented for his past indiscretions, he felt the need to "fix" the mistakes of his children—those mistakes he perceived to be consequences of his own sins.

Each time he tried, he'd meet with nothing but frustration as his attempts continued to remind him of his limitations as a human being. God not only meant for us to forgive each other, but ourselves as well. Long after God has forgiven us, we walk around with guilt.

The "thing" that you've done, which seems to replay in your mind, continues to hold you hostage because you don't trust or believe that you deserve to be forgiven. But that's not up to you. It is your job to ask for forgiveness, and it is God's grace to grant it. And how should you respond once He does? You should gladly let "it" go because God has.

Personal Reflection

What unresolved sin is still keeping me in bondage?

_____

_____

_____

_____

_____

_____

_____

_____

_____

_____

_____

_____

_____

DAY 9

"Now faith is being sure of what we hope for and certain of what we do not see"
(Hebrews 11:1)

About twenty years ago, when VCRs were the DVD players of its day and cost over $200, I witnessed my brother's disappointment in something in which he placed his faith. He came home from work one day all smiles with a box in his hands. He placed it on the kitchen table and told us all to gather around. He'd purchased the family's first VCR for only $50 from a panhandler. He tore through the heavy box only to find about 15 pounds of wet newspaper stuffed in plastic. After sympathizing with him, we erupted in laughter at his expense, of course, literally. He had been had. This did not change the fact that he had faith that what he paid for he would get. The problem with him was not whether he HAD faith but that he had misguided faith.

I once heard a pastor say, "Faith is having active confidence in God's Word. This is the only way to have the desired and lasting results that we seek. It's like placing a mail-catalog order and trusting that the receipt you receive from your credit card company is the assurance that what's on that receipt will arrive in the mail. It's going to the mailbox and expecting that that which you purchased will arrive." And I'll add this, if it has not arrived by the promised date, faith gets on the phone and calls customer service because what you've ordered has been paid for and is rightfully yours. In extenuating circumstances, faith warrants a discount or even additional merchandise to compensate for your inconvenience.

After an intense discussion with a friend, he said to me that I had more faith than he. I don't believe it's a matter of more faith but rather in whom I chose to place my faith. If you walked out of your house this morning, you have faith. If you got in your car, on the train or on the bus today, you have faith—faith that you'd reach your destination safely. Chances are you did not lament over whether you should or shouldn't go out because of concern for danger. And you probably didn't think twice about the route you took. Why? You have become accustomed to this routine. That's simple faith! It is knowing that what is promised to you will be yours. Hold on to what God's Word has promised you and have an active confidence that *it will* come to pass.

Personal Reflection

In whom do I put my faith?

_____

_____

_____

_____

_____

_____

_____

_____

_____

_____

_____

_____

_____

_____

DAY 10

"Trust in the Lord with all your heart and lean not on your own understanding; in all your ways acknowledge him and he will make your paths straight"
(Proverbs 3:5)

Have you ever considered what it would be like if we were created to walk with our right arm and leg going in the same direction at the same time? I tried it for a while and discovered it does not work. In fact, it felt quite unnatural and quickly reverted back to the natural way of walking with alternating arms and legs.

We never question the things we do naturally because we're used to doing them. We walk, run, speak, blink, and cough without thinking about the sequence or even the effort behind each activity. Trust me when I tell you that there is a process behind each—a process that takes place right up to the point of the action itself. Yet, we don't question the process. We simply accept these things as is. The body and every organ in it are designed for specific purposes. Each organ signals another and causes an activity.

Though we don't see it happening, we know it's happening. Why, then, do we struggle to believe God is always present with us? We've prayed for a particular family member's salvation, a friend's healing, or the "ideal" job, to find years later, we're still waiting. And what do we say? "I've prayed and nothing happened." We must remember that lack of physical evidence does not mean inaction.

Take my friend, for example, who had been praying for a loved one's salvation for over 20 years. She called me one day frustrated because that particular loved one was ill and facing death but still had not in her opinion, repented. Instead of seeing God's hand working, she chose to focus on the pain her loved one had caused the family over the years.

After a few minutes of listening to her and asking a few probing questions, I was able to get her to focus on the good that was beginning to come out of the situation. She and the loved one were talking more and sharing stories that they never had before. And though there were some dark discoveries along the way, everyone involved was being purged and healed in the process. I don't know why it had to come to that for the process to begin. I just know that God is not bound by our time. He *is* time. There's no beginning or end with Him. Everything He does is well thought out. He is always moving, rearranging, working, and perfecting His plan in our lives, whether or not it's apparent to us. What feels unnatural or uncomfortable to us has already been calculated into His perfect synchronized plan.

So, just as a healthy body operates without effort apparent to us, let us allow His plan to unfold in our lives—even when it's not clear. Just trust Him.

Personal Reflection

What's causing me not to trust God totally?

_____

_____

_____

_____

_____

_____

_____

_____

_____

_____

_____

_____

_____

DAY 11

"Cast but a glance at riches, and they are gone, for they will surely sprout wings and fly off to the sky like an eagle"
(Proverbs 23:5)

I was visiting with a friend one day when our catch-up-on-old-times conversation turned to career aspirations and eventually, wealth-building. We shared our desires to be wealthy, and in fact, even declared that one day, by faith, we shall be. Suddenly, my friend made a poignant statement, "I don't want to sacrifice the people I love in the name of wealth."

The wealth familiar to most of us comes with a hefty price. It's the kind that most of us envy in our "rich" neighbors—several cars, large homes, furs, and other costly items that, let's be honest, many of us will never possess.

On my drive home that evening, I recalled a conversation I had with my brother many years prior while driving through one of New Jersey's affluent neighborhoods. The homes were beautiful, large, and breathtaking even, but there were no lights on in any of them. I mentioned to my brother how odd I thought that was, and he turned to me and said, "That's because they are out making money to maintain their lifestyle."

What is the point of amassing things you don't have time to enjoy? Yet, many people strive to do so. Certainly there are those who can actually afford these things and have time to enjoy them, but the rest continue to try and keep up with the Jones' without giving much thought to the sacrifices that come with it. Personally, I want to spend time with my loved ones. I want to take time out for me, for giving thanks, and for the simpler yet more important things. I want ALL that life has to offer me, but like my friend, I don't want to sacrifice the important things.

If keeping up with the Jones' is what drives you, remember the lights in your home will soon go out, too.

Personal Reflection

Am I pursuing only wealth and riches?

_____

_____

_____

_____

_____

_____

_____

_____

_____

_____

_____

_____

DAY 12

"…I will turn their mourning into gladness; I will give them comfort and joy instead of sorrow"
(Jeremiah 31:13)

I was at the doctor's office one day when my girlfriend called me with the awful news of the slaying that took place at Virginia Polytechnic and State University. I was dumbfounded. I could not fully grasp the gravity of the situation. It was so surreal that for a moment, I mentally blacked out. Moments later, I realized she was still talking about how the slayer was selfish and mean and should have taken just his life rather than the lives of others. I tried to explain to her that rational people usually don't do such things and that somehow this individual was pushed to the edge. She did not accept my assessment and remained adamant about her position. Then, I reminded her of the plight I faced just months prior.

An unfortunate situation caused me to sink into a depression. Despite knowing that it was not my fault, and despite having wonderful friends and family members who prayed with me, encouraged me, and even cried with me, I kept sinking. I knew I had hit an all-time low when I began having visions of hurting those who had accused me, and destroying anything that I associated with that terrible experience. I kept plotting when, where, and how I might execute my plan. But I had enough love in my life to share what I was going through with my friends who reminded me of the many times I overcame obstacles that I once saw as insurmountable. They reminded me that the Greater One lives in me and that all pain, disappointment, and grief are purposeful. And we prayed and prayed until I overcame.

The point is that each of us has a limit and will be faced with at least one situation in life that can serve as a catalyst to soar or a reason to sink. I don't know the details of what led up to that young man's decision. What I do know, however, is that it could have easily been me. What changed my outcome is my relationship with God and the friends and family with whom He has graced my life. There are many individuals who have nowhere to turn in their darkest hour, and that, to me, is one of the saddest realities of today. Difficulties in life are certain, but one can avoid being consumed by them. As long as there's life, there's hope. If for any reason you are dealing with a situation that does not appear to be letting up, reach out to someone, anyone. Just don't suffer in silence. God promises joy for our pain, and He is a keeper of His promises. Stay encouraged.

Personal Reflection

What in my life do I need help overcoming?

_____

_____

_____

_____

_____

_____

_____

_____

_____

_____

_____

_____

DAY 13

"...Love is not easily angered, it keeps no record of wrongs. Love does not delight in evil but rejoices with the truth. It always protects, always trusts, always hopes, always perseveres"
(1 Corinthians 13:4)

I had the opportunity to see the third installment of *Spider-Man* . Beneath all the special effects and the underlying love story, was bitterness and un-forgiveness—emotions not even a friendly neighborhood superhero could escape. In this particular installment, Spider-Man uncovers his dark side. It the realization that his latest opponent was his uncle's killer, raw emotions were conjured up and some dark, liquid formation, referred to as venom attached itself to *Spider-Man*. His super powers were magnified with a twist of bitterness and egotistic recklessness that became self-serving.

Watching this movie reminded me of so many people who are still somehow managing to exist with deep-rooted and unresolved issues in their hearts. Venom is defined as a toxic secretion, poison, malice, or spite. Animals such as snakes and spiders use venom to hunt for food or as a defense mechanism. [1] Humans, on the other hand, have the ability to direct this force of sorts in a vengeful way, oftentimes waiting several years for an opportunity to inflict harm on those who've hurt or disappointed us.

What we don't realize is that venom was not meant for us to store up. Unlike animals, venom that is kept inside of us and lays dormant, leads to many illnesses and regrets—even death. Letting go is as much for us as it is for the other person. When we forgive, we choose love—love for others and ourselves. Love NEVER fails.

Personal Reflection

Is there un-forgiveness in my heart?

_____

_____

_____

_____

_____

_____

_____

_____

_____

_____

_____

_____

_____

DAY 14

"Surely goodness and mercy shall follow me all the days of my life and I will dwell in the house of the Lord forever"
(Psalms 23:6)

One day while at the cosmetics counter in a department store—a terrible place for idle hands, I succumbed to the pressure of getting a makeover. Business was grim and the make-up artist just needed a project—me. About ten minutes into it, the counter became flooded with women wanting products and makeovers. I could not believe that it was the same counter I had approached just minutes prior. In that moment, I realized how often I've encountered similar situations where my actions sparked a following.

A week later, I heard a sermon entitled, *Jesus Passed By.* The main point of it was, while on earth, when Jesus passed by, things happened—miracles. The essence of the sermon resonated with me because of my department-store experience. I'm not suggesting that I can work miracles, but this got me thinking about what happens when *we* pass by. Do we leave a place or a person feeling blessed—thankful that we showed up? Or do we leave destruction behind where others choke on our dust? Are we living so those who come after us have fewer obstacles to overcome because we've blazed a trail in their honor? Or are we creating more barriers for them to navigate?

Whatever is following us is in direct correlation with how we live. And how we live is a reflection of what we believe and whom we follow. If we are followers of Christ, then only goodness and mercy can follow us. Is there a pleasant fragrance in your wake?

Personal Reflection

What's following you?

_____

_____

_____

_____

_____

_____

_____

_____

_____

_____

_____

_____

DAY 15

"…It is easier for a camel to go through the eye of a needle than for a rich man to enter the kingdom of God"
(Matthew 19:24)

According to economists, everyone and everything has a price. Of course, the initial meaning of this statement had to do with companies developing pricing structures for products where the value for dollar made sense to the consumer. But it seems this is also true when it comes to our morals. For many, everything is negotiable—families, human rights, and even life itself. Sadly, there is no longer a divide on this matter when it comes to those who are supposed to set the standard. That is not to say that each of us does not have a personal obligation to a higher moral standard, but we look to those figures in our lives—our parents, teachers, ministers, and government—to be guides.

I've had several conversations with friends and strangers who have come to the realization that in their pursuit of fame, fortune, and the corner office on executive row, they have lost their families, their health, and themselves. What once seemed to them like ultimate success and the American dream remains illusive, and the pursuit of it has robbed these individuals of other elements that comprise that very dream. This begs the questions: What are you willing to give up in order to realize your dream? Is there anything in your life that is absolutely not for sale? Where do you draw the line?

Personal Reflection

What's Your Price?

_____

_____

_____

_____

_____

_____

_____

_____

_____

_____

_____

_____

_____

DAY 16

"My sheep listen to my voice; I know them, and they follow me"
(John 10:27)

A friend of mine once asked me how I know when God is speaking to me. Quick to regurgitate what I've heard in church all my life, I began to run down the list: His voice is calm and persistent; it confirms what you already know in your spirit; and it brings total peace about your decision. Realizing that I too have been struggling with hearing God's voice, I became introspective, trying to understand what in my life has changed since I last heard God's voice with certainty. It quickly became apparent. I stopped praying and reading my Bible consistently; I increased the activities in my life; and somehow I habitually submitted to every other distraction that came my way. It's no wonder why I'd had difficulty hearing God's voice. The truth is I'd been too busy to listen.

An internet search on "listening" yields over 10 million results, an indication that there's no shortage of theories and strategies for becoming a better listener. Many are the tactics taught by corporate trainers in assisting organizations to become more productive through active listening amongst employees. Interestingly enough, I found a parallel between the insights offered on one of the sites and the Word of God. The site lists the following ways to prepare oneself to listen: focus your attention on the speaker, review mentally what you already know about the subject, acknowledge your emotional state, and set aside your prejudices and opinions. When I viewed these in light of scripture, here's what I found:

Focus your attention on the speaker—stop all non-relevant activities before coming into His presence. In other words, get in position and turn your attention to God.

Review what you already know about the subject matter—know that He is faithful, forgiving, loving, and waiting for you with open arms no matter what wrong you have done.

Acknowledge your emotional state—know that it's alright to be broken before Him, to be sad, lonely, or afraid. He understands.

Set aside your prejudices and opinions—forget how things turned out for you the last time and believe that this time will be different.

Personal Reflection

Am I in position to hear from God?

_____

_____

_____

_____

_____

_____

_____

_____

_____

_____

_____

_____

_____

DAY 17

"Do not merely listen to the word, and so deceive yourselves. Do what it says"
(James 1:22)

It is funny how when we pray and God answers, we seek a second opinion, particularly when it's not the answer we'd hoped for. We convince ourselves that God must have misunderstood us. Perhaps we did not clearly communicate our prayer. So what do we do? If you're like me, you seek counsel from your "most spiritual" friend, and when all else fails, you resort to fasting. Yet, His answer remains the same.

When God speaks, He usually confirms what we already know in our spirit, which is diametrically opposed to the desires of our flesh. In the natural, His answers don't make sense, so we set out to uncover an answer that "feels" comfortable. Many of us, after accepting God's call, live a stagnated life. We struggle with truly turning our lives over to God and with keeping up with our worldly agendas. Someone once said, "Salvation is free, but it will cost you." It wasn't until recently, that I came to understand what that meant.

When God speaks, our answer ought to be a resounding, *Amen*. The difficulty in agreeing with God is that we fear it may cost us everything as we now know it to be. Agreement sets the wheel of destiny in motion to grind away those current things in our lives that are not fit to take into our future. It is the pruning process that is necessary for health and growth. Jesus Christ reminds us of this when He says, "I am the true vine, and My Father is the vinedresser. Every branch in Me that does not bear fruit He takes away; and every branch that bears fruit He prunes, that it may bear more fruit" (John 15:1-2). Pruning involves cutting off superfluous branches in order that the tree bear better fruit, grow higher, or become healthier.

If we hear the Word of God, we must take care to do what *It* says. Doing what God says isn't easy, but we must remember that no test or temptation that we will face is beyond the scope of what other men and women of God have had to face. Be encouraged! He will not allow us to be pushed beyond our limit. We must trust that God has an eternal perspective of our lives, and everything He tells us to do today is moving us toward His divine plan. We must always be ready to listen so that when God speaks, we hear and then "DO."

Personal Reflection

What in your life is causing you not to hear God's voice?

_____

_____

_____

_____

_____

_____

_____

_____

_____

_____

_____

_____

_____

DAY 18

"In his heart a man plans his course, but the Lord determines his steps"
(Proverbs 16:9)

One of the most difficult things for me to accept is that I'm not in control of everything that pertains to my life. I don't do well with unknowns. I need a map, a plan, something, or anything that let's me know what's ahead. Steep hills and winding roads, particularly the foggy ones, make me uncomfortable.

You can imagine my never-ending frustration since life just does not unfold in a predictable way. In my recent past, God dealt with me in a way that was unfamiliar. Where He once shouted, He whispered; where He once was quick to respond, He seemed distant. It was maddening.

When things get spiritually uncomfortable for me, I toss and turn at night, failing to rest in His blessed peace. I pout and throw a tantrum in the mornings when I wake up and find that things in the natural have not changed.

Why is it that we can sit on a train, a plane, or some all-too-dangerous amusement park ride, and trust the people that are in control without even knowing their skill level, yet we find it difficult to trust in the All-Knowing One? Who created those who created the train, plane, and those machines that transport us? You got it—Elohim, God our Creator.

One day during that difficult time period while getting dressed, I noticed snow beginning to fall. Within minutes it began to snow faster and harder. I immediately canceled my plans and resigned myself to staying in and cozying up on the couch because I did not want to take the chance on the winding roads that separated me from the highway. After hours had gone by and boredom set in, I decided to call my sister, who was out gallivanting with her daughters in the mall. I assumed since she had a truck, she was not threatened by the snow. That was not the case at all. You see, it was not snowing in her town or any of the surrounding towns for that matter.

Had I only persevered beyond my immediate situation, I would have found sunshine beyond it. But I gave up too early because I didn't have visibility beyond my situation. We, humans, are only able to view where we are from the lens of our past and current situations. However, God's perspective is from eternity to eternity. So who better to trust with the direction of our lives?

Personal Reflection

How do I respond when I can't see God's hand at work in my life?

_____

_____

_____

_____

_____

_____

_____

_____

_____

_____

_____

_____

_____

DAY 19

"Give thanks in all circumstances, for this is God's will for you in Christ Jesus"
(1 Thessalonians 5:18)

For some reason the winter months weigh on me like an oversized coat. During this time I complain about it getting dark too early, about it being too cold to get out of bed and about it being a drag to go to work. My energy level takes a major dip, and my relationship with God somehow mirrors two people having a silent face-off, with an occasional, "You know I love you, but right now I just don't have the energy to show you." That would be me talking, not God. The truth is my attitude tends to require a major overhaul during this season, and one day I got just the jolt I needed.

One Sunday, after talking with a friend about how we all overlook our blessings and focus on what is "lacking" in our lives, he began to say the words of an old song we used to sing in the Pentecostal church in which I grew up: "Count your blessings. Name them one by one. Count your blessings. See what God has done. Count your many blessings. Name them one by one, and it will surprise you what the Lord has done." [2]

So, I began to count: salvation, God's grace, life, health, strength, family, my job, my home, my car, my church, food, love, peace. I can keep going and continue to be pleasantly surprised at the abundance in my life. Clearly God's abundance in my life (and I'm sure in yours) overshadows anything we may think we don't have. For that, I am grateful.

Personal Reflection

What am I thankful for?

_____

_____

_____

_____

_____

_____

_____

_____

_____

_____

_____

_____

_____

DAY 20

"In this you greatly rejoice, though now for a little while you may have had to suffer grief in all kinds of trials. ⁷These have come so that your faith—of greater worth than gold, which perishes even though refined by fire—may be proved genuine and may result in praise, glory and honor when Jesus Christ is revealed"
(1 Peter 1: 6&7)

One day while driving with a friend, we encountered a major thunderstorm. It was one unlike any other I had experienced before. Trees were falling; electrical wires went down and started fires; and accidents occurred along our path. We attempted to park and find a restaurant for cover. However, we could not get out of the car because there was flooding, and the downpour became a major threat to my hair-do and outfit. So, we decided to stay in the car until the storm passed.

The following day, while on my way to work, the sun was shining brilliantly. There was absolutely no trace of the storm that came through the day before. The air was fresh (as fresh as it could be in New Jersey), and the atmosphere felt alive again. I felt encouraged as I realized that everything works in perfect order, whether or not we believe it. The truth is, the days leading up to the storm were grim and oppressive. The humidity was so thick that going outside became a task. And just like clockwork, the rain came to our rescue, to cool us off and hydrate the earth.

It is the same when we go through the storms of life—those storms that weigh heavy on us, causing us to find it extremely difficult to bear. Just when we begin to feel as if all is lost, the rain from heaven comes to refresh us and to build us so we can continue on our journey. Have you noticed that right after a storm, the sun comes to kiss us and give us hope? So, no matter where you are and what storms you're currently facing, remember that they are here to wash away those oppressive areas in your life. And after those storms pass, the sun will come again. But while you're going through, remember, that when it pours, God reigns.

Personal Reflection

What areas in my life do I need God to reign?

_____

_____

_____

_____

_____

_____

_____

_____

_____

_____

_____

_____

DAY 21

"Be strong and courageous. Do not be afraid or terrified because of them, for the LORD your God goes with you; he will never leave you nor forsake you"
(Deuteronomy 31:6)

In the 1939 film, *The Wizard of Oz*, we found each of the main characters in search of something they thought they needed. Dorothy wanted to get back home; the Scarecrow wanted a brain; the Tin Man wanted a heart; and the Lion desperately sought courage. Of all the characters, I am most intrigued by the Lion.

The trait that is most synonymous with a lion is courage. In fact, the lion is said to be the king of the jungle, as he is deemed the most powerful and respected animal there. Yet, in the film, this caricature of him is more cowardly than any of his costars. I don't recall the film providing perspective on how the Lion came to that state, but I imagine that his experiences up to that point clouded how his view of himself. Isn't that how it often is with us humans?

So often, difficult situations in our lives—whether spawned by a loved one, a job, or someone in authority over us—cause us to doubt our awesome abilities, our essence, and our perspective of who we truly are and what we're made of.

We begin to lose confidence in all that we've been able to accomplish in the most trying of times. The fact that we've overcome a terminal illness, the death of a loved one, the all-consuming coursework in graduate school, or the voices of doubt from our childhood, somehow gets overshadowed by the challenge of the moment. We should be reminded, however, that situations as they exist, don't have to be. We are not powerless to change them. We need only the courage to stand and confront them.

Each of the characters in *The Wizard of Oz* already had what he or she thought existed outside of himself or herself. They only needed a different perspective to realize it. In the end, the very Wizard they thought could provide what they needed was a coward himself, and he did not have the means to grant them their wishes. Only you, with the help of God, have the power and means to change your situation. So, if you're looking to be rescued, validated, and affirmed by someone or something outside of yourself, you too will be on the proverbial yellow brick road that leads to a dead end. Take courage.

Personal Reflection

What's keeping me from having the courage to be who I truly am?

_____

_____

_____

_____

_____

_____

_____

_____

_____

_____

_____

_____

_____

DAY 22

"God is able to do exceedingly abundantly above all that we can ask or think"
(Ephesians. 3:20)

My corporate career took an unexpected and painful turn in 2005. To my surprise and resistance, I landed a job at a university. With this new job came a significant decrease in salary—an adjustment I hadn't planned for.

That life-altering event challenged my cash flow. As the financial squeeze became tighter, I hit the panic button and started surfing the net for yet another corporate job in an attempt to restore a certain peace that comes with having a hefty cash-flow.

Remembering God's Word to me about being still and knowing that He is my source, and having come to a place in my faith walk where I had begun to trust God for divine precision where my feet tread, I reminded Him of His Word. If I trust in Him with all my heart and lean not unto my own understanding, He will direct my path (Proverbs 3:5-6). And since He is always faithful to perform His Word, I reminded Him that I was counting on Him to calm my anxieties.

Shortly thereafter I received a call from my attorney, who had recently represented me in the sale of my home, stating that she had a refund check for me from the water company. I was thankful but thought that surely, this could not be the harvest of the many good seeds I've planted. So, I kept meditating on the Word. I then called my life insurance company to check the status of a policy that I had closed out to switch to another carrier. I was told that it was processed, and I would be receiving a refund check. Now, I knew that I was due a refund, but my understanding was that it would be nominal. I was prompted to ask the woman on the other end of the line, to confirm the refund. I was floored. I even told her that there must be some mistake, and then I heard a still voice say, "Why do you doubt? Am I not able to do even more than this?" Yet still, because of an ounce of doubt, I wanted to see the actual check before I believed.

Here's our problem as believers: we limit God even though He said He is able to do exceedingly abundantly above all that we can ask or think (Ephesians. 3:20). This should be the expectation (without compromise) of every believer who walks upright before God. Expecting the unexpected should be a way of life for us, not the exception. Though God's blessings are not always financial, it was what I needed at that time. Trust Him. He knows what you need and when you need it.

Personal Reflection

What in my life do I think is too big for God to handle?

_____

_____

_____

_____

_____

_____

_____

_____

_____

_____

_____

_____

DAY 23

"Do not store up for yourselves treasures on earth, where moth and rust destroy, and where thieves break in and steal"
(Matthew 6:19)

A few years ago, my niece and I escaped to Aruba for a well-needed getaway. I packed for every possible scenario I could have imagined: snacks for late-night cravings, medicine in case I got an upset stomach or the sniffles, ibuprofen and band-aids just in case I suffer an injury, an umbrella for rain, extra linen in case the housekeeper didn't change the sheets, antiseptic wipes to clean up after the housekeeper, and soap and toothpaste in case my niece forgot hers. Needless to say, my suitcase was quite snug. And in my carry-on bag, there were cough drops, tea bags, an extra shirt and some unmentionables in case my suitcase got misplaced.

Once there and the shopping began, I could not figure out where I would put all the souvenirs I was hoping to purchase. There was no room in either of my two bags. I was instantly reminded of a friend, who accompanied me on a trip to Ghana a few years prior and who had to purchase extra luggage just to store the items she purchased. In addition, she had to pay the airlines for the extra weight. I later learned that once we came back to the US, she gave away most of the things she purchased because she had no use for them.

We wrack our minds planning and preparing for every possible scenario, often missing the grace we have for the very moment. If you're like me, your life runs on a schedule, filled with things to do—a list of tasks that never ends. What is it about ourselves that we don't want to face and that makes us hide behind our schedules and other unimportant things, leaving us no time for reflection or even for God? How can God fill our lives with good things if there is no room? We can over-prepare (or in my case, over-pack) for one thing and be completely unprepared for another. Had a disaster occurred in Aruba, most of the items I took would have been useless.

The bottom line is this: As we travel through life we need to be prepared but not to the point of missing the experience of the journey. Leave that extra room in your bag for the little treasures you're sure to find along your journey.

Personal Reflection

What are you carrying that you don't need?

_____

_____

_____

_____

_____

_____

_____

_____

_____

_____

_____

_____

DAY 24

"We live by faith, not by sight"
(2 Corinthians 5:7)

I've had several conversations with individuals who have been disappointed with certain aspects of their lives. What is disheartening is that these individuals are all Christians. This is not to say that Christians do not or should not ever reach a point of frustration; after all, we are human. Their disappointments seem to have stemmed from unanswered prayers— prayers that have gone up and continue to go up, yet no answer. The petitions run the gamut from the desire of a mate to financial breakthrough to supernatural healing. How does one in a counseling role respond to questions such as: "If God is all-knowing and all-powerful to create the world in seven days, why is He waiting years to answer my prayer?" And how does the counselor respond when she has the same question?

Determined to find an answer or at least some words of encouragement, I turned to several veterans of this faith-walk, and here is what one of them shared with me: We are only privy to what we feel and see during a valley experience. All we want is to get to the mountain top by skipping past all the levels in between. But God has an eternal perspective, and only He knows the exact time frame of our valley and mountaintop experiences. He also knows how we will respond along the way. And quite frankly, if He showed us every step, some of us may well give up.

I thought about God's omniscience and could not help but relate His viewpoint to the eyes of an eagle. I am certainly not comparing an eagle's vision to that of God's, but rather to that of a human being. An eagle's eyesight is eight times sharper than a human being's perfect vision. It can see a rabbit two miles away. Then it hit me, eagles aren't called to walk by faith, *we* are. Hence, God did not give us the physical eyesight of an eagle. However, He did give us spiritual insight to trust that He knows what's best for us. He is well aware of His promises and is faithful to keep them. We may never know why God takes a long time to answer our prayers, but I know that He already knows how it will turn out. Trust His perspective and His timing and have faith that He *will* answer.

Personal Reflection

Am I walking by faith?

_____

_____

_____

_____

_____

_____

_____

_____

_____

_____

_____

_____

_____

DAY 25

"Praise you because I am fearfully and wonderfully made. Your works are wonderful. I know that full well"
(Psalm 139:14)

Countless times I'd been approached by a dear family member or friend who was convinced they had just the perfect mate for me and I'm honored and blessed to have people in my life who think so deeply about me. What's more, they only utter ed words that have floated around in my mind and heart until one day while on vacation.

I had been planning to purchase diamond studs, a purchase I considered to be major. Those who know me well know that when a major decision is before me, I vet it out from every possible angle. I had been told that jewelry, particularly diamonds, are less expensive in the Caribbean than in the US. So, I went to Aruba with a budget in mind and my diamond-stud-analysis spreadsheet in tow. I visited several jewelers and compared prices. The salesman in first store I walked into showed me his selection and asked me how much I was willing to spend. Since discovering one of the keys to receiving stellar customer service is acting like there is no bottom to one's pocket, I simply shrugged. I was quickly reminded that my budget at the time would only afford me a total of 1 carat, so I decided to keep looking. I moved on to another jeweler that someone on my plane recommended. He showed me all he had in the case including one pair that totaled 2 carats for the same price the previous jeweler was charging me for one carat. I thought maybe it was a discount because I was sent by a long-time customer of the store. I examined the earrings with the magnifying glass and found there was a flaw in one of the diamonds. When I brought this to jeweler's attention, his response gave me pause.

He said, "Of course. That's why they're in this case. The more valuable diamonds are in the back, hidden." At that point, I could no longer focus on diamonds. I realized that the diamonds in the case are for common folks—those who simply want to say they have diamonds without regard for the purity of the gem, those who are convinced they're getting a bargain. The serious buyers—the ones who have decided they want quality diamonds, and are willing to pay the asking price no matter how high—are those for whom the "diamonds in the back" were reserved and waiting. These are the diamonds for which a jeweler would rather close shop than sell at bargain prices—no negotiating.

If you're a single woman or man and you know that you have been faithful and obedient to God's Word, rest in your position ("in the back and hidden"), as a treasured jewel that awaits the right buyer to come along and pay for your worth. Until then, sparkle in the back room and pierce the darkness.

Personal Reflection

Am I willing to negotiate my value?

_____

_____

_____

_____

_____

_____

_____

_____

_____

_____

_____

_____

DAY 26

"You shall not covet…anything that belongs to your neighbor"
(Exodus 20:17)

A few years ago while walking down 86th Street in New York City, I noticed from a distance, a woman walking what appeared to be a frantic cocker spaniel. As I got closer, I realized the cause for the dog's behavior. He was attempting to catch a bird that would occasionally land to pick at the bread crumbs on the ground. The dog jumped, barked, tried to run under a parked car, and even got itself tangled around a tree all in an attempt to obtain something he obviously wasn't meant to have.

This scenario is an all too familiar one as it is no different from what many of us do. We exert so much energy in an effort to obtain things that belong to or that are meant for others—a home, job, car, someone else's position in the church. And sometimes we seek after things even after God has clearly given us the "don't-even-think-about-it" finger-wave. All the while what IS meant for us sits on the shelf.

We kick, scream, and try to justify our indiscretions by telling others and ourselves, "God told me this is what I should do or say." Heed this: If your pursuits are causing you to behave like that cocker spaniel, it was not the voice of God that you heard. What God has given others is for them and what He's given you is for you. Be content.

Personal Reflection

Is the glitz of someone else's blessing causing me to lose sight of my own?

_____

_____

_____

_____

_____

_____

_____

_____

_____

_____

_____

_____

DAY 27

"Do nothing out of selfish ambition or vain conceit, but in humility consider others better than yourselves. Each of you should look not only to your own interests, but also to the interests of others"
(Philippians 2: 3&4)

Each year people make resolutions to lose weight, quit smoking, join a gym, etc. More than likely these resolutions will either teeter throughout the year or fall by the wayside altogether. I usually resolve to be a less selfish person.

The reality of my selfishness became apparent when right before Christmas of 2006 a fellow classmate sent me a letter that will forever be etched in my heart and mind. Hers is an experience that would cause most Christians to question God. She was recently divorced, fighting her second bout with breast cancer, dealing with her ex-husband's abduction of her children, and working for her father who penalized her for missing days from work. Still, her focus was on a friend of her youngest daughter who has spina bifida and who is being raised by a single father.

That Christmas, my classmate slept in 22-degree weather waiting for Toys R Us to open so that she could purchase the new Nintendo Wii™ for her children. She would later learn that the mere action of playing the game would help her daughter's friend build upper body strength which could prolong her life, even if only for a few weeks. So, she decided, after consulting with her children, to wrap the gift and give it to the little girl instead of to her own children. Though I'm not yet a mother, I've heard how difficult it is for one to deprive her children. And I would imagine this was not an easy decision for my classmate. Through it all, here's how she summed up her letter: "I may be dealing with what seems like a lot of hardships, but no matter what the docs say, no matter how long I have to fight my ex and his wife legally and emotionally, no matter how much trouble I get into at work, no matter how many doctor's bills I have to deal with for my own children's disabilities, at least I know that my kids are on the right path in life and they will be okay. I also know that there are always others that have a much more difficult path to follow than I and that I am very blessed (a little stressed out, but blessed)."

All of us in small ways can change the world for the better with small acts of kindness. I dare us to look beyond our own needs and see how we can help someone else. We are blessed to be a blessing.

Personal Reflection

In what areas do I need to be less selfish?

_____

_____

_____

_____

_____

_____

_____

_____

_____

_____

_____

_____

DAY 28

"So, if you think you are standing firm, be careful that you don't fall"
(1 Corinthians 10:12)

When something takes a lot of effort and time to achieve, there is often a sense of relief that comes with that achievement. We tend to relax, take a break, and sometimes, depending on what it is, we even go to sleep. However, that moment of relief or act of retreat should never come in the life of the believer, for that is the moment when we are most vulnerable. The greatest pastors and spiritual warriors would agree that after their biggest victories, comes a higher level of attack with more strategies and tactics from the enemy's camp.

Sure, we should pause to celebrate our victories. But our guards should not be lowered—ever. The Great Wall of China, one of our world's greatest wonders, was built as a barrier to keep the enemies of China from attacking it. The completion of the wall was indeed a victorious moment in China's history. However, the wall was eventually penetrated, not by the physical weapons of their northern rivals, but by the coercion of one of its military guards who was supposed to have been "at attention."

As with believers, the protection was there, but the will of the guard was influenced because his position was "at ease" instead of "at attention." Remember this: while our position in Christ has been eternally secured and protected, our position here and now on this earth, should remain "AT ATTENTION."

Personal Reflection

Where am I most vulnerable in my faith?

_____

_____

_____

_____

_____

_____

_____

_____

_____

_____

_____

_____

DAY 29

"As long as it is day, we must do the work of him who sent me. Night is coming, when no one can work"
(John 9:4)

I often find myself in a rut, spinning my wheels and trying to figure out how to breakthrough to the next phase in my life where dreams and aspirations are realized. Determined to break free, I began one day began taking inventory of my life and what I uncovered was startling. At that point I had about three major unfinished projects to which God has called me and at least one significant skill set that I wanted to develop. Each project had some evidence that I'd given thought to it.

At the initial prompting of each project I began with great excitement and enthusiasm. I'd read books, called meetings, and done research to move them forward. In the midst of doing so, I had to balance life changes, work, family, friends, and various distractions that I allowed to take me off course. I noticed that whenever I got off course, I would vow to get back on course as soon as my situation changed. But it never did.

Years later these projects sat idly on the shelf waiting for "the perfect conditions." The reality is that there's no such thing. How often have we promised ourselves that we'd get things done when the children are older, or when we get a promotion and more money?" The English poet, Edward Young once said, "Procrastination is the thief of time and tomorrow is the day when idlers work, and fools reform."[3]

Life will always present us with things, people, and situations for which we did not plan; and if we sit around waiting for the right conditions before we act, we will never move forward. I cringe at the thought of leaving this earth without having accomplished that which I've been sent to do. None of us know how much time we have. Whatever you were sent here on earth to do cannot wait.

Personal Reflection

If my time on earth expired today, would I have regrets?

_____

_____

_____

_____

_____

_____

_____

_____

_____

_____

_____

_____

DAY 30

***"Let your light so shine before men, that they may see your good deeds
and praise your Father in heaven"***
(Matthew 5:16)

It seems that Christians are among the greatest turn-offs in our society today. It has become more popular for us to brag about our faith than to live it. We fail to notice that the louder we speak, the faster people run because our talk is not consistent with our walk. How can we speak of God's love and not show it? How can we admonish our children to tell the truth at all times yet command them to tell the bill-collectors we're not available? We've become repulsive to the very world to which we are called to be salt and light.

Recently, my niece was surprised to learn that some of my friends are unsaved. In fact, some of them believe in other gods. She thought it was odd that I, being a strong believer, would have friends outside of my "Christian world." I had to correct her, gently. The truth is she's not alone in her thinking as most Christians seem to think that we should only have Christian friends. However, this kind of thinking flies in the face of the great commission of Christ, which instructs Christians to go out and make disciples of ALL nations. How can we do that if we hide in our Christian comfort zone?

Folks are tired of the Christian blab and are looking for us to model the way instead. My friends are my friends first and foremost because of our love for each other, which according to the word of God, bears all things. The best testimony I can give is how I live, and in doing so, hope to plant seeds along the way.

There is nothing attractive about a Christian who engages in Bible-beating an unbeliever. We attract by loving others and living a life that is indicative of the Christ in us. I'd rather see a Christian than hear one any day. St. Francis of the Assisi sums it up well when he says, "At all times, preach the gospel, and when necessary, speak."

Personal Reflection

Am I a talking head or a walking testimony?

_____

_____

_____

_____

_____

_____

_____

_____

_____

_____

_____

_____

_____

DAY 31

"Do not be deceived: God cannot be mocked. A man reaps what he sows"
(Galatians 6:7)

When I was much younger I use to watch my mom tend my sister-in-law's garden. One day she called me over to boast of her handy work, but I watched from a distance because I have an utter disgust for worms and mostly anything that crawls or slithers. I noticed her struggle with some weeds that invaded the garden. To her, they were bothersome, but to the untrained eye, the weeds blended in with the plants and flowers. Nonetheless, she was not pleased with the way the garden was taking shape.

I absolutely love flowers, plants, and most anything that beautifies the earth. Yet, my fear of worms and garden snakes threaten to keep me from ever taking part in what people like my mom find very therapeutic and rewarding. I can only admire from a distance, which means I may never become an expert at gardening. However, a simple truth that even a gardening reject like me knows is that seeds produce after their own kind. It is absolutely impossible to plant an orange seed and get an apple tree.

If you're not seeing the results you expect in life, perhaps you need to tend your garden. Might you have planted the wrong seed? Have you allowed weeds to choke out what you've planted? What about the garden pests? Did you use the right repellant? And what about your soil, did you use the right fertilizer?

Now, we all know I'm not talking about actual gardening. I'm speaking of words and actions that we sow into our own lives and those of others. Every word you speak or action you take can determine the type of outcome you experience. If you want your garden to look like peace, to smell like love, and to taste like joy, then you have to plant those seeds. Unlike an actual garden which stays fixed in one place and goes to sleep during certain seasons to regenerate, your garden is always contending with the elements of life (weather, work, people, etc.). This gives you more of a reason to work at planting those seeds that render your desired outcome.

As for the weeds, when you begin to take note of your actions, the pruning process will begin, and soon enough, your garden will be a work of art.

Personal Reflection

What seeds have I planted?

_____

_____

_____

_____

_____

_____

_____

_____

_____

_____

_____

_____

_____

_____

Bibliography

http://www.merriam-webster.com/Johnson Oatman, Jr., in *Songs for Young People,* by Edwin Excell (Chicago, Illinois: 1897). http://thinkexist.com/quotes/edward_young/